The Big Melt

President of the United Hearts

"We have seen the best of our time:
machinations, hollowness, treachery,
and all ruinous disorders,
follow us disquietly to our graves."

Sc. 2, line 11 *(Othello).*

The Big Melt
President of the United Hearts

PS3577
Factory School, 2007
ISBN: 978-1-60001-988-3

The Big Melt shadows the ruinous disorders of American politics and war mongering from three weeks prior to the 2004 US presidential election through three months of corruption following the election. Private and public literary and political correspondence and conversation, among various other literatures and media are at play in the poems assembled, and more-or-less as dated.

The map on the cover is a cartogram of the 2004 US presidential election results prepared by Michael Gastner, Cosma Shalizi, and Mark Newman at the University of Michigan. See http://www-personal.umich.edu/~mejn/election/

President of the United Hearts gratefully acknowledges the editor of *antennae* in which a handful of its ambiguities previously appeared.

Factory School is a learning and production collective engaged in action research, multiple-media arts, publishing, and community service. For more information please visit factoryschool.org.

TABLE OF CONTENTS

The Big Melt, 7

Forward by Giorgio Agamben, 71

The Big Melt

"Say to them:
Man has survived hitherto because he was too ignorant to know how to realize his wishes. Now that he can realize them, he must either change them or perish."

— *William Carlos Williams*

October 12, 2004

Take me in to the world
You sit down. You read. You develop.
Leave unfinished the task of peace
Which redeemable business
Pleasure and privation, arrogance
A universal ruined suspension seduces
The contingent sweat in maddening
Unmitigated hate – the vanished assets
Dropped in the green and rancid.
You bastards!
It's crazy, the society's generated
"We don't know what was already known"
The fixed feature, i.e. the 'truth',
I.e. the final resting place –
The greenish ink on the editorial:
America, you can go anywhere!
Procedures no longer accept
The natural stone, the systematized
Will rendered impersonal
Will be detached from where it began;
Metrical and have meaning
We're kidding ourselves
The stewards blend to confirm
The runoff comprising the stable
Heads of lettuce, the risk adverse
Men walked on too many angles
Recipients carve up flesh
"Not to worry, don't panic, the revolution
Dwells on precisely nothing
In nice quotations 'involvements'
Its heirs ephemerally lend
No dead lines or addiction
But solitary renewable machinery
Soluble embarrassments and foreign
Exquisitely provisioned
Powdered, tenacious and dull
Promise of success

October 13, 2004

The gift of utility in time; the gift?
The ceilings of the rooms, the furniture
Out of the house-like equilibrium
Cannot whether through letters or
Through acquaintances turn it off
I'm going to turn it off
The churching senselessness
I need these fingers to write my sentence
You're going to leave in an hour
It's not fair I didn't get to play
It's a step and a retreat gradually
Gaining control
Losing a mother, a daughter,
A relative or even a friend
Or a past
Pastime
Even the trees have doubts
Their remains capsize into the positive
Inprofitable shame
The entertainment?
Like you, I stand in doorways adjudicated
By romantics and sentimentalists
Competitors expert in the businesses of life
Decades-old flames of apolitical
Discontent – its biographers
Exquisite craft coming to worship
A social arrogance, eating
Its hopeless instantaneity
Having become the art of what is said
A comparative history
Implacable consequence of
Commemorative 'brutal beauty'
The poor groping for the solvent door?
A cup of coffee? Men who have not
Received what they deserve?
The synergy of space?
How much of it is real

Where are these world-shaking plans?
The cheerful thing?
Is that the first truth?
Maximize profit and lead us through anguish
Startlingly odd but implanted
No longer held alien or unfixed but together
A tremendous system of traps
You walk in
And that's it

October 14, 2004

Nothing here but in the feral
Evolution
Introduction
Protocols it's taken ten seconds to destroy
Solitary and renewable similitude
Another page
Rancid debt in the definitive and
Authentic
A scheduled intermediate
Barter and gift
Ornamental softness at its tips
A stop-motion ambition
Blueprints in the prow
Push the beloved stinking shit hole
This warm deconstruction
Might well go shout at the moon
"We are the synergy of anguish,
Look what's on my head"
The good neighbor policy, tit for tat
Doesn't matter
The coming diminishment
Will not utterly destroy the upward
Mobility of the disadvantaged?
This is the letter 'l'; 'l' is for 'land'
Press a button,
You sit down. You read

I can already see where you're going
The sacrificial
Composure and sobriety
A wavelength
Oh joy, rapture
The light doesn't matter

October 17, 2004

To be ruled by imperialism and prayer
Money might shout
At the moon
I confess just now – it doesn't seduce me
Between assets
Abandoned
Whole towns dismantled for pennies
A renewable decline
In the green soil
In the poverty ground
Where are you?
You're going to ruin it; can you do that?
Recipients no longer
Repelled
Faith-based asymmetry
Somersaults
The 'nature of things' a lunatic
Complement and futility
These houses are built to burn down
[We can go slower if you would prefer]
Contradictions?
The wrong contradiction
The wrong politics
The wrong science
Where do you want the oil first?
Why don't you get your finger out of the way?!
I have so got brains!
I'm not afraid of anything!
You sat down. You read…

You didn't understand what you read
Growing our dicks [in a sarcophagus
With single malt & oysters]
Let's talk again soon
I'm not your slave
Better attuned to the infinite
I never host an event without crystal
It takes seconds
To destroy my attention

October 17, 2004

Bang on my chest if you think it's perfect
Some one faxed this in
At the half-way house
Nasty! A man made out of tin!
What do you want?
The practice of freedom?
Fuck "knowledge" as one-upmanship!
Fuck you fucking bourgeois assholes!
Fuck power and hierarchy!
Fuck you and your ultra-sensitive "ideas"!
I'm fucking crossing over, I'm making
What's yours fucking mine!
You fucking don't like it, do you!
Fuck you if you don't like it,
Fucking shitheads!

October 18, 2004

They begin to set up readings
In parks and restaurants
And in neighborhoods the ventriloquist
Speaking through their mouths the abandoned
Thought of a very small cow, the honeymoon
Of the world break their lease

October 18, 2004

Gentlemen, I think it will get darker
Before it gets lighter, is my nose bleeding?
Undeniably dead but attractive
We'll get it right this time, won't we?
Do we have to go in? [Expletive]
Forests stink of the failure – what country
(Is it his?) Guarantees complete
Excretions that moisten that
Potential or incomprehensibility
Nature produces comparable to
An invasion that cannot be
Its scheduled no-show disregard.
It's impossible to be an artist
The point of deception
Complete control, pretending control
An attentive eye, the open ear
Allegory heavier than rock
Lynndie England and her leash
Go blindly to disaster
Clamped to his genitals
The giant ice shelf splits asunder
"People scare better when they're dying"
This society's crazed
Covered with straps they could not
Stand being free
In the vernacular of the peasantry
Society's unmitigated hate
Looks like a "whopper"
Isolates matrixes gummy 'eligibility'
Inadequately equipped environs
[A persistence of catastrophe]
Build up and never evaporate
Undeniably and reliably
The human body will be an event
This is your cake, and this is your crown
You can go anywhere
The final resting place

The patented ink in the editorial:
We killed each other
In bursts of mud

October 20, 2004

This dinner party fails the county test
The pending lawsuit, except for the flag, is dark red
A rotting mound of Christian & Muslim
Dispensing inexpensive pamphlets
Primitive universals the bombers betray
Men and women kissed in the peripheral
Irreparable protest – bedding, mattresses,
Living rooms couch, chairs, bathroom linens
Tossing the carpet between tomato cans
New alliances a sacrificial layer
The dead the multiple panes
Of intellect serenely transverse
Boiling a two-minute egg I could be wearing a
Lame smile too, escarpments blunt
Always meant to look up
The thought of the conflict, outcomes
Outermost nerve placed under glass
From the inner shell gassed
Unfinished anvil, compromising
Perception or fat travesties
Rub of peeling flesh the parentheses
Jerked in from the hillside
Lines introverted inside;
You're going to bed the lie now?
The dispossessed constituent trustee
Covered by the pitching lip
Alive in the bottle it came from
Political canasta unravels
The mind to rhyme marketing its time
Unconditional refusal
Doing its duty the shifting idealized
Bearish or bullish shrift

Implacable unprepared
Smaller than a wavelength
Peopled one by one
Hung on the erotic ignorance
If you push me, I push you
The voice-over can take anything
The heart and soul at the bottom, uneducated,
Poor, no longer has to fake it
This dinner party fails the county test
I like the one with teeth
The original homogenization in the hidden
Calcium outfitted with an exercise
Bicycle even after death

Coda

I need these fingers to write my sentence

Place the grenade in the column you want to destroy

My future may not involve so drastic a metamorphosis as you've described. Having never been the size of a bear or bull, I hope the coming diminishment will not utterly destroy my debonair deer-like self.

The upward mobility of the disadvantaged
Gaps, gravitational resonances
Ubiquitous patent of phony
Motorcycles, bikes and pushcarts
Prohibited in an attempt to avert
A half-unconscious bitch

Coda 2

"the vilest of whores"

Broken nouveau-riche napoleon

These words rhyme
Can you follow me?

I didn't make any changes

Strategy (like prayer) is an impassioned
Equilibrium

October 20, 2004

A less than responsive peace force
Pit bulls? Even art instructors can achieve
Interdisciplinarity. At the same time, however, she is also
A free and secure citizen of heaven, for she is also attached
To a similarly calculated heavenly chain. Thus,
If she wants to get down to earth, she is choked
By the heavenly collar and chain; if she wants to get into heaven,
She is choked by the earthly one. And in spite of this
She has all the possibilities, and feels that it is so; indeed,
She even refuses to attribute the whole thing
To a mistake in the original chaining
She says, 'mistranslated circus of personal ambition'
He says, 'monumentalist high-modernist motivations are unveiled'
She / he says, 'characterization means sales'
He, on the other hand, 'attempts to waltz the night away'
No one says what do you want to eat?
No one says the unusual secrecy is hurting children
No one says the headless body sleeps in a cold bed
I think it would be nice if you shared all of it
Tell her you'll share

October 21, 2004

Food is noted as "necessarily subjective," with
"No hard and fast rules"
Someone, they say, turned fish…or was it
Something else into fish? Who baked the bread?
A tiny piece of food that fell on the floor
It's all politics, the grunts say
Why don't you throw that in the trash now?
Wipe your face and hands
Bless you…the premises under which we went to war
Have been proven to be fallacious
(AUDIO GAP) it's very important you have to listen
And this is a very frustrating can
We admire the way they've dealt with their family
And drink, also little is dead it is dollar also buttery
Buddha spiffy skater on flat
Half melted, also ring the smart their doorknob
Paragraph the radio the put, is across
And becomes, machine is ran? And lonely,
And beyond is twisted CD is killer bee
Is wing she jackrabbit the funny baby there wall?
Their underneath, there yellow she rose painful
Overcooked their mine are out

October 21, 2004

I didn't make any changes
The individual utility generated
Editorialized systems of
The stable solitary tenacious cap sized
Ornament of ambivalence
Everyone could be "rich" somewhere
The indentured immensurability
A "reverse technique" that wouldn't accede
You're so modest you can follow your
Broken nouveau-riche
Uneducated polemic

By the modest scale of what it means
To be greeted and free

Take me into that world? I see opportunity
From the air – anything that comes up
In the generic "weekend" of creativity
Might not generate but fashions
Celebrations cycling counter-clockwise
Props investment and drill
Transcribes speculative cash flow
Beneficial to this street? This factory?
The school? This "business-plan"?
Being poor eats up all my time
I'm doing exactly what I shouldn't be doing
Initiated through zero and "entitled"?
I want fruit not a fanatical
Compassion speculating in market
Speed and philanthropy
Close your eyes – you didn't see anything
How much training do you need?
[To use it would be really interesting]
Is it wrong to force a man to masturbate?
I didn't see it, this mirror shows
Anything that you wish to see
The gloves are coming off, gentlemen
You are no longer my prisoner
Everything is going just swimmingly
I know he looks vicious but he's really kind
Just how big was the beast?

I feel like an astronomer seeing
In another galaxy the open pages of a book
On black voodoo power and witchcraft
This isn't working
He's as crazy as the old man

October 21, 2004

Unmitigated vanished dropped
Severe dead run ground sprinkle pray
Subject impassioned computerized
Sense advertising against
Crazy generated fixed wonder
Don't know already know
Silence stripped habits ego
Constructed introverted said place
Lived have become pat kind implacable
Comparable rise instant consequence
Eating brutal beauty solvent
Heat subject sufferings
Real synergy space groping
Door big impact establishing general
Seconds destroy want attention
Another solitary renewable
Verisimilitude fled memory fanning
Sweat rancid debt relationship
Definitive shift nostalgic authentic
Scheduled lines backs toil
Day day out intermediate
Ornamental softness tips hat
Ambition personal top-motion filled
Coke another murder type
This accident tells real blueprints
Prow ship destroyer events state it
Perpetrated invisible audience decades
Another completely apart
Longer relationships
Repelled asymmetry faith-based
Somersaults turn initiatives
Nature thing lunatic symmetry
Penal institutions dead sarcophagus
Perverse futility compliments
The houses bread winner
Right time we do we go in time
Expletive forest stink failure country

Is guarantee disregard complete?
Footholds excretions moisten
Potential incomprehensibility
Invasion cannot imitate produces
Point deception dispossessed from
Be silent perhaps bottle constituents
Political unraveling body empathy
Put drawers meaning angles
All sums worth owning translation
Edge fascinating examples
Mind began rhyme mind marking time
Marching its unconditional

(2)

Similarly calculated heavenly chain
Thus wants get down earth is choked
Heavenly collar chain wants get into heaven
Choked earthly one spite this has possibilities
Feels it is indeed refuses attribute whole
Mistake original chaining (AUDIO GAP)
It's important have listen is is frustrating
Cancer admire way dealt family drink
Little dead dollar buttery spiffy skater
Flat tender half melted ring smart doorknob
Paragraph radio put across
Choice mentality fascism generate fashion
Celebration cycling counter-clockwise fashion
Props up investment drill transcribes speculative
Cash flow beneficial street factory school
Business-plan exactly what shouldn't doing
Doing being poor time being eats up
Initiated zero entitled want fruit
Dealt drink little dollar dead

October 22, 2004

The right to resist one's own survival?
Is't not possible to understand in another
Tongue? How if I answer "no"?
Between compression
Working native perennials into existing
Plant community, get'n food out of it too
The brass have repeatedly
Demonstrated their disregard
Have engendered a justifiable outrage
Your recent matches
Fill me with shame
New product families inside something else
Acted as one man just figured out
Half of my image walking ahead responding
To my thoughts of victory and
Irreparable loss an entire black outline
Of cultural history? Of incessant pain?
A few months after that
Dust on the white dresser
Quest delayed at least 20 minutes
They are using a pack of wolves

October 24, 2004

Everything becomes very cheap
You are on call and you don't know when you can go
But the tickets cost a fraction
It's difficult to contain my concern
Who spoke on the condition of anonymity?
Look at me, she said, there's got to be more than this
There's just got to be
Fire your sleep gun, listen
Very well, show them in
During this sorrow
Listen...
"I am life...I am oblivion...I am love..."

Their language when they speak
Is on another beloved
When buy-in becomes everything
The war will change
Its scheduled appearance fled what we wished to see
The lease breaks open
Mouths split asunder
The "something else," the "comfort line"
Read in full decline
Is implanted but held together
Walks in accidents seduced by the thought
It won't get into any trouble
You can follow counter-clockwise
It's perfect
The mirror will show you the whole thing
To achieve a fair share
Possibilities have been calculated
"At the top you no longer have to fake it," it says
"At the bottom, let's talk again soon"
The editorial? We're kidding ourselves
American society's always
Infinite periphery
Attractive to the eye
And free
Standing in the sentimental
Sacrificial
Not afraid of anything

October 27, 2004

Globes of fire placed under glass
The inner shell unfinished and promising
Mr. Sidebottom, it's after school and it's wet
My yummy, yummy toe
Seed activism promises renewable imprecision
Their cheerful attention
I'm going to come over and make you
Smack your head on a rock, said

Mr. Sidebottom (Guess his wife's on top,
The mad strategy in the ground
The dropped unmitigated ego the runoff
Carving up words or lettuce
Or addiction of an upper class not
'Fraid of anything rendered relevant
Relative to the manufacture or protocol
To destroy semblance or original
The vanished asset says
The son-of-a-bitch woke me up!
We're going in our toy house for one
More minute…it's cold out…
I'm sorry we have to go, we might need
Your help to transition
Walk Whitman
He never knew what hit him
The whole world was saved
By the smallest of all
Will you please go now?
What will happen is up to the reader
Be subversive as hell

October 27, 2004

A trembling portion more important than
There's no fucking arguing with

…The intellect of dead alliances?

…"The post love world"?

The astronomer looks vicious in any language
I'm not your slave, you dick!

"Pink pink a cool bam groove note air breath"
To burn down futility

Bending hints of all the world's sunrises and sunsets
The heavenly choked by the earthly

October 28, 2004

Who is the No.1 lollipop of the U.S. Senate?
Constituent Lives in Bottle
It's been right in front of us for a long, long time
"Dear, it can't be that hard
To come back
The way we came"
You're going to bed inside whose lines?
It's so hard to think different...
The greeted pompous and free
Get sneezed all the way across suckerland
An imagined resist to right one's own survival
They might laugh at our weakness
A friend relates to something from Emerson –
"Part of self-reliance is to protect other people from you"
What did it really mean...?
Do not become caught up
In the particular identity of the work
The shadow in the alien
That won't step down, that won't apologize
Follow me everybody
(These resources just don't make sense)
Patronize representation ceremonially
Reluctant ceremonially peps speeded armistice or aliening
Or stunts take me into the world
I'm making a door right over this
Paramilitary's boastful lack lumbers surge damages
Actionless reluctant
Fun loving, armistice or dilemmas degenerates
Bequeath refinement reluctantocratic disability
The role of social communication
Those that retreat to
That won't think
Conquer and the whole Empire says, "Well done!"
And not only do the masters place
Are all done by officials?
Murderousness
Scrum

Ferryman
Toothbrush
Trinities
Suprasquamosal
Unriveted
Glowworm
The best revolutionary
Moron, the dinner, our pigeon, is
Made out of tin

October 30, 2004

Free and secure citizens simply, quietly
Melt away
Hopelessly caught in the goop
The more turbulent bloodshed
Serenely transverses
In a form of ornamental and intermediate
Personal ambition
Lent to an outcome hung on
Implacable unprepared
Invisible destroyers
Leashed in the prayer-like groping for the door
The class war goes on
But I haven't heard my friends
Concentrating
That compression seems too far-fetched
The oobleck in every heartbeat
A clammy and accurate design negative alibi
One billion dollar per is difficult to find
A kind of free enterprise
It's your world of creeps
Thought or thesis singing songs whose popularity
Perhaps despite wildly different styles
Can hurt, choked by
The heavenly collar and chain
An assumption traced
Within the credentials of your own class

Played against the ceiling
Surrounded by the uselessness
Requirement insists on –
In tumbling parties dead folk evaporate
Indentured servants put to death
Emotional compatibility
Consumed faces north
To erase the story
The world that broke its lease
Cycling appearances in trim clockwise
Thimbles of mentionable ill-gotten
To rest on top the scene
The neighborhood neglected
Dangerous and unstable
Emptied, enveloped, inelegantly sawed off
Some say, as it was meant to be
Possibly forever
Too cold to open or close anything

October 30, 2004

You don't know what you're doing
When you woke a different liquid
Filled your cup, invisible
Clumped on the countertop
The bread that fell on the floor
The first truth is the most penetrating
I'm not afraid of anything politically
I didn't make the deception
A bracketed invariance
Crack or delaminate the deferred
Distinguished in speech
Providing the introduction
I know it looks vicious but
It's an apple in the trash
The freshly baked
Reappear, male or female the head
Is in synch with the room

Its singing mouth dissonant
Unraveling in mud the body
Asserts in an oobleckian sequence
A monumental mistranslated
Word fishing for what is not
Pruned in the educated
Universal suspension
The contingent sweat in the mad
Unmitigated world
Thousands of screaming
(Nothing there but in the periphery)
Leaving the war
The great living neutrality
Having disappeared
The flat tender absence
Inexpressive half-melted
Penetrates compassionate
Its baked foam sputters...
"From now on I can call anything
The name I invent for it."
It spoke, "For I no longer know
What I am speaking of..."

November 1, 2004

Start over. Sit down. Read. Develop.
Change, change it to one. No. That's right.
No. That's right. That's right. Goodbye.
Even my remains capsize into the positive
A man in military formation not personality
The onset of general poverty for all?
Charlotte Rampling or Charles Manson?
Title for zeitgeist: 'Oobleck' or 'bootlick'
Just be happy you're not a lampshade
(This will work if you take the fangs out)
Anything can be used as an excuse
Here in Coconut Grove we denunciate
His lack of education is more than

Compensated for by his keenly developed
Moral bankruptcy – the smallest of all
Alliances in the perimeter of lies
The window for peaceful settlement closing
Lies outside his jurisdiction
The "fraudulence paradox" of "Oblivion"
Expressions of ignorance or at a minimum
Great naiveté – public space or "place"
Taken "inside," to project into it?
To force a man to masturbate?
One's mind is its unconditional refusal
To achieve a fair share ill-gotten
In complete disregard undeserved
If you think it's perfect and soothing
To the smell, where are you?
Get on the damn bus doorknock
Take me out of the world you'll ruin
My inner animal won't step down
Won't apologize, follows me everywhere
There's just got to be anonymity?
Exceptionalism? Selling the scrap steel?
I don't think I'm going to get to vote
The antiseptic wants supplying, checks
Deputies of the illiterate without shred
Of encouragement – the supremacy
A prologue and denouement pierces
The impeachable slack

November 3, 2004

The raw vote numbers top the expertise
A problem among bread winners
People weren't really paying that much
Attention to were anxious about
The pessimist plan or Election Day
Trying to figure out what's going
Numbers and base absentee ballots
Irregularities icon too many litigate

Too many states the cynicism and despair
The vote in process should, it's clear
At last meet the end? Won't forget
Outcomes of the conflict but the thoughts
Fall though I write in my head everyday
Among democrat and republican
Peoples have gone to the poll
The Cuban thing didn't work out, she never
Calls me back – I think John Daschle's
Coming back…it broke very, very late in
1998, even Kentucky, South Dakota
Depends on justifiable disregard
Is his brother happy Bush won Indiana?
I thought you were going to finish
Those sentence another way, a multi-million
Put a key phrase in their chairmen
What are you concerned about, what are
You worried about tonight?
Let's make sure everybody gets in
Where are you? Take it into the world
Setting the state for democracy
And post-election challenge
Sixteen states about to close winners
That colossal closeness margin
Reports are encouraging, cautiously
Optimistic urban vote counted
Ohio, particularly when you look at
New Mexico it's now a tougher hill
Let's see if that happens 98%
The possibility of an error is so small

I thought people wanted change
The strategy ran words in the ground
Sprinkled mistreatment like prayer
An impassioned dilution
The linear and passionately felt
Fictional smear marginally did better
Pessimism must make a greater effort
Assimilate up to 200,000 votes

Democracy, privation, and arrogance
What else do we have to do? Devastation
Horror in over 78% of the precincts
"Tonight doesn't seem a very good night"
The instant and hostile consequence
Everyone's focused to a second term
Guns god gays the pantheon elected
What provisional are we living in?

This is a thesis paper, not a book

The air is inked with cowardice

November 3, 2004

The older we get the more we layer over
It's the club of identity and of mediocrity
Why not hang up a sign: "No poor people allowed"
To step outside the identifiable, to refuse
More Americans voted against George Bush
Than any sitting president in history

The almost blissful absorption induced
By this suspension

The big melt has begun

November 19, 2004

Some are disappearing already

The aristocrat
The artist
The bohemian
The foreigner
The immigrant
The minority

The poor
The remnant

Dissonance having found its representative
Of dispossession

Let her have five minutes on the couch
Then it will be our turn

Narrative hunger?

Either you have the chair
Or you have the cat

You do not choose

What is it?

Four and one-half...
Four and three-quarters...

Bent bodies writing in time, light, space

Five

November 21, 2004

A twist in black and white
The runoff of renewable imprecision
Smacks your head
His keenly developed lampshade is closing
This mirror will show you what you wish to see
She wants to get down to earth
Do you want to eat?
The hillside hopelessly introverted
Has bled
Your slave understands what you read
I didn't get to play like you

The reading is half melted, the reading
Can take anything from the air
Its tough thought eats up all time

November 22, 2004

Its source is everywhere

I'm all for being deliberate, but sometimes
I'm not

November 23, 2004

A survey Monday by the Norway-based Fafo Institute for
Applied Social Science said that since the March 2003
Invasion, malnutrition among children between the ages
Of 6 months and 5 years old has grown 7.7 percent
From 4 percent

Years of sanctions, tyranny and war have crippled the
Country, and even before the latest conflict one in every
Eight Iraqi children died before the age of 5

Lt. Gen. Lance Smith, deputy commanding general of the
U.S. Central Command, told reporters in Washington last
Week that humanitarian assistance in Fallujah was being
Provided by U.S. military forces, Iraqi security forces and
"Other humanitarian organizations"

He didn't elaborate, and relief organizations based in
Geneva said they had no idea which humanitarian groups
He was referring to

November 26, 2004

What do you think I'm doing right now?

What watt wowed foil another occupied swat
Linked work link an operative no go neologism proofed
Spewed fizz spot spoken
Were beamed outage spiff deliberate furtive cheek
Juice jinxed oxen

What I wish to see is closing

I walk straight ahead (into a periphery

The relationship to memory, cultural & individual
Has been stripped

The half-melted
Can't stand being free

December 2, 2004

I can taste the world with my feet
My thoughts have become segmented
I will not melt

Could you help me lift my feet up to my nose?
An abstract expressionist snowman –
My gut instinct is it needs another twig
How 'nothing' became 'next-to-nothing'
It's all about the weather – I'll give you one more chance,
One more chance and that's it
Push the "metamorphosis" self-narrative
That potential incomprehensibility –
Through their mouths the abandoned
Thought of the very small:
When I was your age I sat there nicely
Not any more

Nothing but the machinery
Hints of all the world's sunrises and sunsets
The door seems too far-fetched
There is the renewable decline by the smallest
Of all – the outermost gassed by the inner
The master's disability the oblivion
Necessarily headless, solemn, peremptory, emotive
The insolent grace and brilliant prolixity
The muted warmth and intimate vibration
The wild and flashing simplicity
Not from but *into* the world – its unscheduled
Appearance a sort of cosmic respiration
An engulfing void, a riot of color
The sacrificial Iraqi and American
Covered with an equal light
Voted against the suspension –
Its extremely delicate "accommodations"
Its invulnerable guile
Its exhibitionist ostentation

December 4, 2004

We're beamed offstage, rendered virtually invisible. Under "all the Circumstances," that mania for loci, for documentation. Community and Conversation draw on the artistic laws of creation—though disintegrated, Annihilated and dissolved between the social processes of exclusion and The process of selection by which some are designated important, others Not, and that of a more backward telegraphic availability of what was Once an area of privacy protected inside the external traditional relation (a Persistence of catastrophe) but now traced into the interior.

Even before the latest conflict, the common surface of the same thought, The anonymity becomes very cheap. The sacrificial and free want fruit for A dollar; exclude most of their more radical if not complete excretions. Implacable, unprepared and leashed in the prayer-like and reliably poor let People underestimate you. The exculpatory production wants homes not too Dumb to maybe not know what its saying. The refusal is more than death.

What we really do value? There are birds singing deterrence walking
Down the drain and laughing. Hard to hold, its meaning is grasped again
On re-reading. Our conception of causality is incapable of explaining it.
You can follow counter-clockwise and drill the mirror to achieve a fair
Share. The future peace smells of that ditch. Its unconstitutional
Steadiness becomes a revision of the post-conceptual "Once upon a time,"
The scheduled simplicity of it.

Here it comes, the unimpeachable lack.

December 5, 2004

Ý¦»¦»‰»ë»é»á»Þ»¹Á£»Þ»ÀÁ¢»»èï?»ëÇ¢ÇÇÇ¦Ç—
Çé»Ç»Ž§¾»ü»'»¹»ô» ®»ëŸËï„»è?»¹»'"•™Á"˜»è»¤»®»‰Á¢»»èï?
»¦»‰»ë»é»á »Þ»¹Á£»»èï?»ìÁ¢»»èï?»ëÇ¢ÇÇÇ¦Ç—Çé»Âô'?
I'm afraid we're too late, and must prepare ourselves
For more invasions (and if privacy exists, selves exist, at least
Their behavior!). We won't forget the outcome of the conflict
Though the thought falls away. Process is with us, moving
Out of the past already vanished into the future yet to come,
Nourishing the present with the transient qualities the organisms
Are marvelously created to enjoy. Ownership that does not
Wholeheartedly participate or demonstrate the harmony of the
Process becomes an exercise in "control," the individual
As "slave driver." Indivisible destroyers and leashed in prayer-like
Expectations stars trip and squirm inside the community in
Dumbbell's window. The right hand hasn't seen the left hand
In years; sawed off, some say, possibly forever: "I like the figments
Of my own fantasy better than the triviality of material reality."
This is the calm precise mind of luxury, a ceremonial catalogue
Of the undefined. The ill-measured, in preference for the clinging
Sweetness of incoherence, directs the popular orientation –
A space where dead folks collect and build up and never really
Evaporate. So much for inconsistency. Confused by the scale,
How are we meant to read this, or view that?

December 11, 2004

The window is closing, it's perfect and soothing
They resist the changes rather than embrace them
Its ornamental softness eschews the dispossessed
The impeachable pierces their supremacy
This mirror will show you my prisoner is more than
Compensated – let people estimate
What is said is illiterate
Tyranny and war have crippled the country?
My thoughts are with you, though
The heavenly collar and chain falls away
Let them throw a wide pass to center
The loss leaves home in an invulnerable heart
Its scheduled vibration
Is the ruin of our souls

December 12, 2004

What if I freeze out there in front of everybody?
You can't tell me what to do
Insolent mice! It's impossible to cross the sea of storms!
Surely you don't want to spend the rest of your life
The size of a mouse?! Who's there?
The transient identity of the work won't apologize
We'll fix this right up
How come you can't listen? These walls
Are solid ice. Who's farting?
I escaped before being crushed only to die
It's beautiful, the snow isn't even cold
Soon it will all be a memory
Well, what news do you bring? You're looking
Especially regal this evening
I didn't know things had gotten this bad
What are you doing here? We're both victims
Of magic – you're forgetting that I am your superior
And I'll be in charge of the expedition
The trick is making you useful, what does one create

When one has everything
Kind, clever, and brave – rock that will walk
Destroy who I seek, destruction and havoc
Will be yours to wreak – find the wooden man!
Sleep seems kind of pointless
You're the bungling clodhopper whose leadership skills
Put me there! Why don't you invite him
For tea and cakes while you're at it?! Look,
He'll break right through, you'll be pulverized
And saved us from a vicious pile of rock
That is what you want, isn't it? This one doesn't
Have a happy ending
One more minute's a very short time
No time to enjoy the scenery
Are you coming?
There's no way off this island.
Are you sure about this? Okay, let's go.
I want this to be an unforgettable show –
All is right with the world – it seems your subjects are
Intent on uprising. If you don't hurry,
You'll spend the rest of your life as houseflies,
Or was it horseflies?
I can see her but she can't
See us; or hear us. That rat's got to be stopped –
Is that any way to run a kingdom? There's more to being
King than wearing a crown – those peasants
Who do challenge me living statuary let them be. I'm afraid
I underestimated. Dismemberment or barbecue?
Your mouth is still much too big – smaller, smaller you will be.
Don't worry, I'm just wood, remember?
It's difficult to contain my concern

December 12, 2004 – in memory of Jackson Mac Low

Remorse of being, of not being there

We light the Hanukkah candles –

You brought visible order to chance

You let poetry happen

You usher us to the present

December eighth, two-thousand and four

We love the whole world for its very uselessness

The poem has fallen asleep, Jackson

Wake us up!

December 13, 2004

In the bestial frenzy of insatiability
Americans in flight escape the melting, fearful
Greeted and free to fake it; at the bottom
They had nothing - after all, they had seen
The end of the world
Had lived through it to comprehend
An inordinate, extraordinary cornucopia
The sacrificial bedding, mattresses,
Are you being psyched out by the waves?
You are no longer gentlemen

God rests his soul
It stands out sharply because of the end of it

The voice of those who suffered
Displayed our own feelings

In Sabbath splendor
You win the dinner
Your friend is mistaken

"Blessed" in the poetic process of appropriation

Sit in your chair or I'll have to take it
I'm glad I voted for you
Everyone tells me you're moving at a snails pace

There's only one present for you to share

I'm going to eat the whole thing

December 13, 2005

Are present only on the edge
Unmitigated, vanished, computerized

A dinner at a fine restaurant rides on its reply

I despise symmetry

You're not getting in my way
Let's put the symmetry back in

I'm going to come over and make you
We love symmetry

If you draw a line down the center
And if you folded me at the line?

Structures of feeling aren't meant to continue
Take off all of your clothes

Transcend the embarrassment

The conflict to make it more suitable
Fights democracy

Limiting to a strategic line
The melted, mistranslated, and monumental

Why don't you throw that in the trash now?

Wipe your face

A sarcophagus
It eats up all time

December 15, 2004

Cost of the war in Iraq as of 11:24pm
$150,295,154,046

A blank of needles will circle memory

And coffins ship out with the jobless

"You were the blue colored wind.
All the ancient animals were returning.
It was always the end of the world,
and the beginning of something beautiful,
but which demanded everything
of everyone."

'Did I commit murder?'

'Is God going to forgive me?'
'How am I going to be when I get home?'

'You won't forget us, will you?'

I am in heaven, killed by
The virtuosity

Vulnerable enough to be opened
In such intimacy, I suffered

The severity *matters*

December 18, 2004

In ghastly alternation, says the
Iraqi girl, 3 or 4 years old, her skull torn open by a stray round the
Kuwaiti man imprisoned for 13 years by Saddam Hussein, cowering in
madness and covered in waste the young
American soldier, desperate to escape the fighting, who sat in
the latrine and fired his M-16 through his arm the Iraqi
missile speeding in as troops scramble in the dark for cover "That's the
one that just stops my heart," said Mr. Brown. "I'm in my
rack sleeping and there's a school bus full of explosives coming down at
me and there's nowhere to go." As of Wednesday
(December 15, 2004) 5,229 Americans have been seriously
wounded in Iraq. Through July, nearly 31,000
veterans of Operation Iraqi Freedom had applied for disability
benefits for injuries or psychological ailments
"We still have a long ways to go," he said.
"The warrior ethos is that there are no imperfections."

December 31, 2004

First the sentence, and then the evidence!
"Mr. Hughes strikes me as having been an exceptional voyeur,"

"The need to lend a voice to suffering is a condition of truth."
Hans Burkhardt

So the Platonic Year
Whirls out new right and wrong,
Whirls in the old instead;
All men are dancers and their tread
Goes to the barbarous clangour of a gong.
W. B. Yeats, "Nineteen Hundred and Nineteen"

Do you think it isn't true?

You are a book
You are a big book

I'm going to write
On you

December 31, 2004

And now those who drown
Being taken inside

It's this very complete human experience

Please come back again
Chance carries everything
Away

January 2, 2005

Some things are not meant to continue
When they speak our inattention
Has fled what we wish not to see
No time to enjoy the scenery
They had nothing
There's no way off this island
Are you coming?
Are you sure about this?
The almost blissful absorption
One's own survival speculating to right
In speed and philanthropy
The cap is closing – close your eyes
I didn't see anything smaller
I live in the bottle it came from
Please pass the salt
Its unscheduled vibration
An anthropo-psycho-epigenetic wave
How come you can't listen?
Long-term billows whipped up
A huge circulatory system

We're beamed offstage on the bottle
Annihilated and dissolved

A sort of cosmic respiration
An engulfing void, a riot
You're going into the sea? For whom?
You sit down you shit
It follows you everywhere
Disintegrated
Mere material, really and completely
That is what you want
To have a happy ending
Isn't it?

January 3, 2005

We know more now
That the perception won't last
Sometimes confrontation
Sometimes stereo, sometimes choral
You want to argue with it, slightly out of focus,
You want to read it a second time
Nature's lunatic symmetry?
A lack of "maturity" can be a valuable asset
One's life is expired in song
In this context cannibalism can be productive
A practice of oobleckian invariance
To crack or delaminate
The beloved cathode on another poet's page
Conserving the best of what one has
Your utilization ratio
Can be taken out of the transaction
There are no imperfections

January 4, 2005

In the earthly chaining
An Emersonian "self-assembly"

Opened by drops in elevation
Scale-indifferent
Translates master and peasant

Caffeinated
Peaceful
And alone

Everyone, along with the environment,
Disappears

January 4, 2005

Nothing takes your life
An incomplete transition of thought composed
The composition of incomplete transitions
Not both? This must be the longest
______ I've written to anyone in a long time
Contemporary 'retreats' and 'returns'

From a time long, long ago:

Falling apart

Writing is traveling to the land of the dead to steal home.
The key lies in the black ink that flows from the pen,
A pen admired for its simple inefficiency. It inevitably runs dry
And one begins the revolution again, coming home
A prize under one's arm – mementos momentarily possessed.
As with the music of Miles Davis, of Debussy each single bit comes
Of its singular accord with nature.

January 5, 2005

Clouds of steam blanket the traveler
The half-melted oxen choked on its tongue
The freshly baked head appears in foam

A voice puts out the flame
The "grammar" of the whole distilled
Into articles of sand, the screw of the future
Pulled by faint molecular interactions
Is known to have little more than
A superficial engagement with culture
The conservative country club canon
New product families delayed
All the assumptions behind yet another institution, sadly
With all that entails, based in New York City,
Is just about too much
We're going in our toy house to never

The foam on one's tongue
Faint molecular flames
Crushed by snow
How easily thoughts stray –
Being taken "inside"
It's your thought
Or thesis, a kind of free enterprise
Being put to death

In India elephant keepers train baby elephants to stay put
By tying a rope, with a stake on the one side, around one leg
And placing the stake into the ground. The baby elephant pulls
And pulls on the rope to no avail. This teaches the elephant
That no matter what he does he cannot get away when attached
To the rope. Later when the elephant is grown up and the keeper
Wants the elephant to stay put all he does is to tie a small piece
Of rope on that leg and the giant elephant is held to the spot
By his own mind.

January 6, 2005

Pleasing no one but themselves
All the muscle-boy lobbyists and politicians
Become professors and the darlings of professors
Teaching the young to revere their muscle-boy law

Because it is good for them, and pure
Teaching women and Jews and queers
To make this muscle-boy law, too

There everything has been edited

Except for the androgynous-looking
On the diving board who are about to
Dive into the space between them

They grow little by little, piece by piece
Didn't make any money

I think she's made it

Gonzales' ballet sealed beneath
A tourniquet of recurrent expertise
Premonitions representative and flesh
Crushed and exalted in bald advocacy
Critique virtue's vulnerability
His victims' beauty

Let her have a minute
To erase the story

January 6, 2005

"Putting this unique metaphorical focus (and its underlying principles)
Into action draws upon military and sociopolitical milestones
To highlight the surges and slides of history"

I couldn't salvage the language or redeem a thought

The waves have cut through the composition of the atmosphere
In weather, earthquakes, and volcanic eruptions – in the arts and business,
And their tributaries

The miscalculations of those who hesitate to intervene?

How much love and care is visible?

To throw oneself out of oneself, to reserve that
To reverse that creation of survival

The young ones are listening in and suddenly come

The final showing up
Can hurt

January 6, 2005

The trees have doubts

My remains capsize into the positive
Unprofitable shame

January 7, 2005

The genetic word made flesh
Stripped and sacrificial

Don't talk to me

Everything you say turns into poetry

January 8, 2005

Save your breath

You don't know what love is

It's that I don't know
It's that I'm unsure

January 10, 2005

Who, among the poets, will ever be like that again?

It's that you don't know
It's that you're unsure

Form melts the page

January 13, 2005

To the possibility that poetry
Stands out sharply because the end of it

The voice of those who suffered
Displayed our own feelings

Are you being psyched out by the waves?
You are no longer gentlemen

The more turbulent bloodshed
Personal ambition and ambivalence

The freshly baked penetrate the room
It's going to eat the whole thing

Keep thinking on that

The tenacity and purposefulness of it
Things you could actually talk about

To reverse what survival
The outcome of the conflict?

This level is more than good enough
Its form melts on the page

It's that you do know
It's that you are sure

Remains capsize into the positive
And profitable shame

January 14, 2005

Dispensing inexpensive pamphlets of protest
Gravitational influences of the planet's moon

A rotting mound of soldiers
Rivers of dust and ice

The fight felt promises salvation
Words meant something more than they do?

In accordance with the law of a million changes
President of the United Hearts changes

What happens may provide something else
It is always present, like the Milky Way

In the particular identity of the work
You can no longer step back

To roam alone is emotionally unsatisfying
The heavenly is choked by earthly relief

Forgive us; it grows little by little, piece by piece

Gravity pulls the strategy to the ground
Mouths unraveling in a layer of mud

Thinking the mouth meant something
Dissonant *and* sentimental

(Maybe the world wanted them in equilibrium)

"I hope the leaving is joyful
                    And that I never return"

The open pages break their lease
We admire the way they've dealt with pain

The indentured immensurability

January 15, 2005

My emotional investments have withdrawn
So much composure and sobriety

To have thrown oneself into it, to reverse that
To serve each with possibility, each word
  cell, meridian, wave

Based on hundreds of candid interviews with barbarians
To bureaucrats at leading publishers and universities who
Have achieved their goals and joined the inner circle,
The Big Melt lays bare the unstated conventions that govern
And shape literary corporate to non-profit hierarchies

Taking readers inside classrooms and private offices to learn
Firsthand how the top decision-makers view and assess
The employees under them, it offers invaluable advice
On such career-building tactics and skills as getting noticed,
Networking, persuading others, knowing which battles to fight,
And mastering the art of the quid pro quo

For all those who aspire to be part of the decision-making
Body of their discipline, *The Big Melt* is the ultimate
Intelligence report on whom to trust and whom to watch out for,
How to manage the inevitable conflicts that will arise
And how to read between the business (and literary) lines

I can't see what this is

January 15, 2005 – to Robert Creeley

What I enjoy is the unfolding
Paying attention to the space one's in
Its grammar emerging the minutia
Can't make up everything
Language pulls a scak or sack over one's eyes
See what I mean? Torture
Becomes, as they say, problematic
I wished to tell someone but couldn't
Until I found my way in
Once there, the idea became clearer
Their presence (those previously relocated)
Made possible its articulation
Putting the idea forward in their absence
It appeared incapable of an assertion
No context and therefore no content
A lack of gravity, or a greater gravity
Nothing could be made of it
Invariably I would attempt to toss it
(Discovering late that I had
Its portability taunted me)
An improvisation in which discipline
Each time I sat down to work
Needed to be counter-balanced
(Subverted) by freedom, to break off
When not needed, or could help
Understand when people
Didn't understand the purpose in
Approaching the conclusion
To press out the last drop
Each time I had to relearn
They had been once beautiful, dangerous and
Unstable – in the wrong time and in
The wrong place
But because they were on all sides wrong
They were right for me

January 17, 2005

Broken
Into small pieces

Dated from the first word
Or from the end of an initial draft completed
A democratic forum of free opinion
Unbelievable

It's amazing how much some people
Are blissfully unaware of how stupid
They really are, says Patrick
To SpongeBob SquarePants

You taste like sponge cake
You ooze fashion

Learn how to feel again
No sentiment included

I called you a stinky butt
Pour some soapy in my bucket

Can you see that I'm very busy?
The answer is, no

Swish your hair in the fresh water
I'm making a door right over this

You too have to sit on this side

You monster, you're getting us cold
Get as much as you need

I don't want that up there, it's too heavy
Tell her you'll share

I say, go

Be really careful with water
You are just really starting to aggravate me
I own it

Get out, right now
Get out

You hear me?!

Everything is wet
The way they've dealt
With their family

Get in your room right now

What am I going to find?

I'm going to tickle you
And you're going to scream

You're wasting a lot of time
This is your crown

Okay, that's too loud
The book is not about them

Fish drink a lot

That is all we got in the camp and it was disgusting
Face me, face me

They arrive in New York dried out and tasteless
It is always disappointing
Also insanely expensive

It lost its place a long time ago

I'm going to sleep by myself tonight
But you sleep right there

January 18, 2005

It's okay to be happy
Even with less than expected

We don't have any kind of accountability

We are faced with globalization
The heart and soul at the bottom, educated or not
Has to fake it

We're talking about torture
It isn't a question of speculation

We'd like to enlist your assistance
In whoopin' your ass

January 19, 2005

The dwindling pipelines of new little dead
Dollar flat tender half melted ring
Starts soup by cooking potato skins
Tastes the world with its feet
Keep your personal overhead
Walk straight into war looking vicious
But being really kind
Dispossessed perhaps bottle deception
Raw portable empathy
A translation worth owning sums
A political climate no more
A 'sinkable remnant' asking trouble
"Respectfully supporting those decisions"
Of a gov't with which one disagrees
A miserable ________ that has no choice
Put that in your new ______ sandwich
Everything's stinky

January 19, 2005

What can you possibly say to avert it?

Annihilation

Crushed, whacked or worked by a wave
The lip of that gnarly bomb

"An inauguration of invulnerable guile

These must be balanced
Understanding the relationships
Immersing oneself in the "doing
Reducing their overall quality of life
White flight and suburbanization
Interpreting the events

I'm going to spread my jism all over your hotplate
Blow chunks or show a Technicolor yawn

Reviewing what has been
Blue tile becomes fashionable
Everything becomes very
Cheap

Serial nation wreckers
A blank of needles

Butt Breach
Cactus Juiced
Carrots

The figure below shows the second loop for learning

Yellowed from compression people concentrate
Inside its examination

January 20, 2005

The alchemy is a one-way street

Falls among democrat and republican

Opens and closes house
Winter and spring

Another important motivation
Contest organizers offer an opportunity
The designer wants everything to be perfect
I have no clue who wrote or when

Deputies of encouragement?
Confirmation?

Its emotional arrow

Assmunch

What actions should be taken
(e.g., diverger, converger, assimilator, accommodator)

When progress is noticeably going well or poorly;

Or when a crisis occurs that disrupts

Follow counter-clockwise and drill
The mirror will show

(Later on, or perhaps never)

the possibilities

January 20, 2005

They have no concept of sacrifice

I want you to be happy with what I do
As a bystander or as a courier
You are on call and you don't know

Though the thought falls away
Out of the already vanished into the
Yet to come, nourishing ______ with
Transient ____________.

Are the organisms qualities …?

The ass has repeatedly
Demonstrated evil disregard

Can we play for a little bit more?

Love songs have faded, the skies are free

Their tumbling flights and the carcasses that
Sidewalks have washed away

No bigger than sesame seeds

Hordes tunnel up from their resting
Shed their skins and take flight

It can hobble the small

"People were worried that everything was going to die"
You travel around the cycle, you begin

(I tried to leave the complex ones out)

You can't afford to

January 21, 2005

How low could it go?

We study surveillance as possible
Interpret the Apocalypse, the Last Times
The inevitable evils, the outside
Its strong ethical component
In the perimeter of lies
The peaceful settlement is closing
Or lies outside a jurisdiction
The "fraudulence paradox" of "Oblivion"
Of at a minimum ignorance
Taken inside to project into it
Collisions ocular propensities

There is nothing worse
Than this pretence of perfection
(That would improve your performance)
A free-market society is too meta-reflected
You don't know when you can go
And the tickets cost a fortune
By staying in the middle, Teflon coated
Values are revised as needed
Shedding light on virtually every
Chauffeur

The curse of incompetence
Thousands of screaming beings
Leaving the world to go into worlds
Having no opportunity to modify
What spirit inhabits them or how
Futures watch life savings
Drain away
From one experience to the next
Manufacture of a protocol
Set to destroy

The scientific entropic paradigm

"Renaissance," "renewal," and "spread of liberty"
Are sometimes used in its place

January 21, 2005

Less tangible factors:

"They don't love you anymore"

The smallest of all

If it's your thought or thesis, a kind of free enterprise
For a world of creeps
Hung on the implacable unprepared
Invisible
Designated as 'location efficient'
(You know how smart these people are)

Begins with a "dirty" interior of red, followed by
A general pattern of more turquoise as it spreads away
We often think that humans are immune to the lunatic instability,
Mistake, cancellation, admiration, drink, ring, fashion, celebration,
Cycle, lock, prop, investment, drill, transcription, benefit

Like at the end of the day
Its unconditional refusal to achieve
That what we do here on Earth
Has effects that go beyond a common
Destruction of life

The U.S. economy has a significant
Impact on the Sun, but sunspots
Have no influence on the economy

The "vanished asset"
The "something else," the "comfort line"
Theory claims that they result from repeated impacts
But I question this ignorance

Of upper class shrift
Its contradictorily similar yet dissimilar
Dependence

Let's play dead

January 25, 2005

A lack of gravity, or a greater gravity
Light sweet crude

The body so thin
Barely exists
The sustenance through which it sees
Its representative
Doesn't have
A happy ending

You folded me
At the dissonance
Sanctions, tyranny
And war

One more fat state
Will stop the flow

The election result
Spiraling upward
Shows you what you wish
Lays out the philosophy
Of close friends

Social mobility beaten, shocked
Persons in custody
Justify ill-treatment

My genitals

Lack of evidence
Were arrested without warrant

Enterprise and ascent
Reopen the crucial inequality

Nothing passes down

February 5, 2005

Oil is a portable climate (no more)

Inside its compression
Hell is
Exothermic
And has already frozen over

A no-other-choice-project?

Note:
But do they listen?
They don't listen
No, one has to scream at them

The difference between art
And military imagery?

Our gross income is asking for trouble

"If you ever come back we'll kill ya!"

All souls go to Hell

February 8, 2005

A 'singable remnant'

"What is your brains' name?"

Some that we find interesting include
This, this, and this

If you stop throwing I could help

Walk straight into war looking ______
But being _____ dispossessed ______
It's hard to think what was meant
The runoff renders irrelevant the new
Reinsertion of neutrality – the mad catheter
Or addition (addiction) outside the verifiable
This interval that we find interesting
This, this, and this
Little by little, piece by piece
The whole world saved, is too numb to
Maybe not know

February 10, 2005

He must either change the *m* or perish

Is this what you'd meant to attach?

"I'm in my rack sleeping and there's a school bus full of explosives
coming down at me and there's nowhere to go."   As
of Wednesday (December 15, 2004) 5,229 Americans   have been
seriously wounded in Iraq.   Through July, nearly
31,000 veterans of Operation Iraqi   Freedom had applied for disability
benefits for injuries   or psychological ailments

I'm in my coming down
The cowering in the young

Freedom had applied for disability benefits
For injuries   or psychological ailments

He'll break right through, saved from a vicious happy ending
The illiterate encouragement

The houses we do not go in
The wood shedding

February 25, 2005

A single sheet of paper

The whole world

We love the book for its very uselessness

We love the whole world, however,
For its use

Anger – Beauty – Lament
Loss – Love – Pain

Bereavement

Pain angers beauty, lamenting the loss of love

To leverage something   (perpetual)
Its repetition

Light, sweet, crude

The perpetual motion
Fixed in its perpetual

Decompose

Touch me. Don't touch me. Touch me. Don't touch. To put my feet...don't touch it. I only want. Don't. Touch me. Touch me. Don't touch. Put your fingers in my pants then...touch me. Don't. Not there. (Perpetual) No. Not that way, here...touches me. Don't touch it. I don't...never...you...it would be...Don't do it. Don't. Here. Touch me. Don't you dare? I told you. That's not what I meant. What did you? I said, don't. There, not there. Yes. But I don't like that. For as long as I can. [Perpetual) When? In the days. Who was it then? No one. Don't. No, none. How can you say that? I hadn't known. It matters though. No. No, it doesn't matter. But your mouth is...I can't. Please. Please? It comes and goes. But everything you've asked for

Prelude to Death

I didn't make any changes
Strategy x is an impassioned square
An unredeemable and arrogant
Individual utility
Generated in editorialized focus –
The stable solitary tenacious capsized
Ornament of ambivalence

Darkness – exclusion – delusion
Educated and fundamentally cruel
Ham-handed, contaminated
Exculpatory refusal

Home health care?
One bedrooms go for $3100 a month
I'm getting $7 an hour

We lived in Bush's America
A ventriloquist abandoned

Universal adversary
The revived (sic) committee for
The clear & present danger

In Nazi Germany
In Stalin's Soviet
The air is thought to be inked
With cowardice

Homelessness, half-light
Remorse of being, of not being there
The perpetual motion of
Search fixed in its perpetual exile
Decomposed oblivion

Notes on Genesis: March 25, 2005

A deeper season
Than reason, we're all of one piece?
Voltaire observed "it's dangerous to be right
In matters on which the established
Authorities are wrong."
Emancipatory denial
Home health care?
War concentrates inside the compress
The flag is more than death
It's clam-like prelude to perception
To everything you've asked for.
You can make it all up yourself
You don't need magic
You've cleared up the truth in a very short time
Made up your own if you've wanted
(You can't take somebody else's)
Are we supposed
To take something with us?

Someday you'll be a fine artist like ______

I'm fine, I'm fine
And we hope that you are too

FORWARD

An Elective Dispatch

By Georgio Agamben

Translated by Karen E. Pinkus
with Mimi Miyagi

The *Big Melt* is a collective's assembled response in verse to the 2004 U.S. Presidential election and its aftermath, i.e. the continuing elision and transfer of legislative power to the executive branch (that vast monument of fatuity leaning toward the future like the Tower of Pisa, in which nothing less than the happiness of humankind is being worked out) in every public sector, government, finance, educational, and cultural. That said, it has been mentioned with a measure of confidentiality that I intend to honor that President of the United Hearts (hereafter, PUH, pronounced *pooh*; a pleasant enough alternative to PUS) is a collective absent the flesh and blood members needed to sustain collaborative endeavors of whatever kind. Be that as it may, PUH's message, urgent and indispensable, is one of gravitas and moral outrage – it is against the radical right and the misguided timidity of progressives. Further, the work generated within its membership comes from its source, the heartland, the opening zero, the Midwest – the void it is roomy to lie in. In action against the philosophy of *myself*, *I*, the correspondences between PUH's eyes, mouths and ears, however arrayed, pushes what is ours upon ourselves, cultivates its promise in our hearts – no measuring its innermost play. As voiced by Medea, "but I was rendered speechless / and from there nothing but pain." PUH is capable of taking the abyss of its own communicability upon itself and of exposing it without fear or complacency. Its promise is a bold move to which the reader no longer viewing life from behind the screen of her ego but able to see things in the human word's return (*nostos*) to splendor willingly succumbs.

Of course, very few people see it. There are few to notice. That's not so bad. Our bodies reside six thousand miles distant from our hopelessly outdated history. The writings of contemporary *American* poets treat words like trade names, and their texts are, at bottom, a form of prospectus for enterprises not yet off the ground. They exist in the space of "cross over" into advertising, so also into the realm of the obscene, leading to no major artery and terminating in no center. Everywhere war plays the starring role in a secularized space—a representation created entirely by the book, yet so widespread as to make up part of the collective mental atmosphere: the abyss of knowledge and of meanings. There's no place like home. What if the collective PUH *is* under siege, or question, or interrogation? What if the collectiveness of identity, in a kind of subsidence of material reality, is being or has been dissolved, fragmented, sheared back to reveal the set(s) of characteristics once complementary but today no longer experienced in relation to one another?

What determines the resistance of a human being?

In poetry the world's dissonance has its representative. Indeed, in the poetic environment formal and semantic relationships are not symmetrical in all directions. Poems (and by extension poets) are generally far more concerned by the social text in front of them than by its detritus an equal distance above, below, or behind them. However, and perhaps more important, when moving a given distance *between* poems, lines and words, one always travels *through* other poems. Although within its bounds a discrete poetic-place may be substantially similar to analogous prose-places, the relationships among poems are vastly different. Three features are particularly salient: distance, adjacency, and fixity. For instance, the relationship between two poems in *The Big Melt* can easily shift based on how one arrives at a given poem, or through the passage of time. The point is to demonstrate the "harmony of the process" – notions of process and existence presuppose each other. In Buddhism, this is the concept of "conditioned genesis" – the unity of any person or thing through time covers an ultimate multiplicity of momentary states or 'flashes' of reality. Individual poems along with the rest of nature are constituted by activities and occasions and their relations. The individual who enjoys a poem is creating it in the process of that enjoyment, working as any other organism to synthesize what is relevant in the environment with which it interacts.

This philosophy presents a moral attitude toward nature by teaching that there is nothing in the universe that is really and completely dead, mere material. Without an appreciation of these features there is nothing to read, is there?

How much of it will you bare?

Every broken door signifies a worry or a hope, every grassy knoll hides an enemy rifle or the IEDs of an invisible and silent insurgent. PUH believes the last stage of a world-historical form is its *comedy*. Somebody has farted very slowly. The gas lingers. We can see the background now because we did not see it then in the comedian of a world order whose *real heroes* are dead. "Why does history follow this course? So that mankind may take leave of its past *gaily*." Karl Marx, *Der histrische Materialismus: Die Frühschriften*. What then?

President of the United Hearts, the collective responsible for this work of dissent, lives in the American Midwest.

Other titles by President of the United Hearts:

County Farm Blues (Past Perfect, 1985)
Nickel's Worth of Liver (Liquid Press, 1990)
Don't Lie Buddy (Past Perfect, 1991)
Pretending I'm Happy (Acrobat Books, 1994)
Your Daddy, Metathesis (Red Bank Road, 1996)
Fat Cat (The Big Dig Press, 1997)
In the Bottle (& under surveillance) (Liquid Press, 1998)
Asking for Trouble (Acrobat Books, 2000)
Crack House (Fashion Label, 2002)
Home Depot Chainsaw with Sound (Pig Pamphlets, 2004)
Acceptualism (The Big Dig Press, 2004)